R·Y   P·O·I·N·T

ANTARCTICA

The continent of Antarctica is a a huge domed ice cap varying in depth between 6,000 and 12,000 feet. The surface of this dome forms the largest and highest plateau in the world; and roughly at its centre lies the South Pole.

At the beginning of this century the unspoilt wilderness regions of Antarctica were still unexplored due to their inaccessibility. To reach Antarctica the explorer must first voyage through the most remote and tempestuous seas on earth. The first guardians appear - huge flat-topped icebergs, some 20 miles in length, drifting northward. The ship enters pack ice – a belt of frozen water, broken into a mass of floes and must thread her way through this for up to 400 miles to reach a wind-swept stretch of open water where massive white cliffs of ice rise from the depths.

This is the coastline of Antarctica...it is a continent of mountains, furrowed valleys and plains – but they are hidden by the tremendous mantle of perpetual ice and snow. Only here and there do peaks and the outlines of rocks rise from the wilderness.

It was to this frozen continent that Discovery came in the early days of the new century and her story of courage, inspiration and adventure began...

Much of Antarctica was discovered and mapped out by British sailor-explorers. Captain James Cook ventured here in 1772. The British government funded an Admiralty expedition in 1839, led by Sir James Clark Ross who discovered the sea and ice shelf which bear his name. Another British probe set off in 1872 when HMS Challenger steamed across the Antarctic Circle with orders to investigate the seas around the new continent.

The National Antarctic Expedition

The Challenger returned after 4 years with a mass of information but it was 17 years before John Murray, a Canadian scientist who had sailed with the ship, rose to address the Royal Geographical Society in London, in November 1893.

Murray gave an electrifying lecture on what he thought lay beneath the frozen wastes. He suggested the time had come for man to cross the interior plateau to its heart, the South Pole.

Listening to Murray was Sir Clements Markham, President of the Royal Geographical Society. Sir Clements was a dominating, forceful character and he set to work to raise funds for a British National Antarctic Expedition.

It was the age of adventure.... a new century was about to dawn.... and newspapers were searching for exciting stories for their readers. Sir Clements knew the value of publicity and soon he had secured handsome contributions from industrialists. He raised £45,000 in all and the British Government matched the sum.

THE OBJECTIVES OF THE EXPEDITION

What had begun as a scientific quest was already being seen by some as a race for the Pole and British pride. But Markham was a serious, cautious man. He wanted no rush for the Pole and carefully recorded what was expected of the expedition – magnetic surveys, oceanographic, biological and physical investigations and researches. There was no mention of being first to the South Pole. Markham also stressed that whoever led the expedition should not be after glamour, but should be someone with a deep sense of responsibility, such as a first-rate naval officer. He set about finding such a man and a suitable ship.

Specifications of the S·H·I·P

A ship committee was formed in 1899. The ship would have to be wooden, due to the amount of magnetic observations it would undertake, and it would be the first built purely for scientific research and Antarctic exploration.

But where could such a ship be constructed? Wooden shipbuilding was becoming obsolete. There were few yards left in Britain capable of building a wooden ship to the exacting specifications demanded of the ship's designer, William Smith.

Tenders were invited and the one from the Dundee Shipbuilders Company, which had long experience of building whaling ships, was accepted on December 16th, 1899. As a major whaling centre in the 19th century, Dundee had a reputation for building strong, wooden ships to withstand the savage conditions in Arctic regions. After haggling over the tender, the construction price was fixed at £34,050 plus £9,700 for the engines. Various other extras would bring the final price to £51,000.

A Whaler at Dundee

Admiral McClintock, Chairman of the Ship Committee, described the new ship thus :

"The Ship will be 172 feet long, 33 feet extreme beam and will be 1570 tons displacement. She will be built of oak and elm, with an ice casing of green heart. Her bows will be sharp and overhanging and they will be strengthened for forcing her way through ice. The full power speed of the ship will be about 8 knots. The plans and designs approved are those of a vessel which will be, by far, the best adapted for severe weather and ice navigation, as well as for scientific investigations, that has ever entered the polar regions....."

The keel was laid on 16 March, 1900 at the Panmure Shipyard, Dundee.

City of Discovery

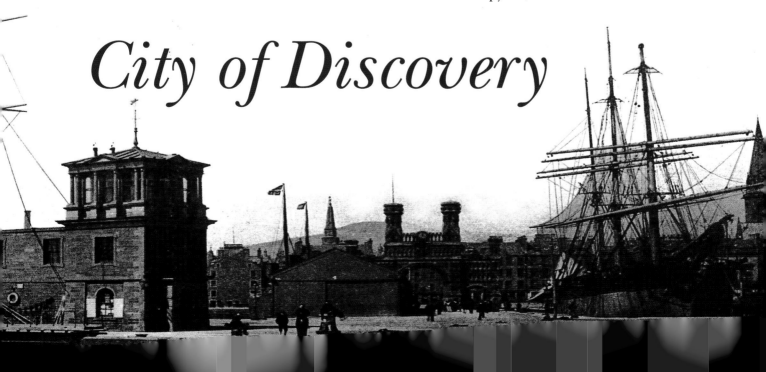

THE LAUNCH OF
Discovery

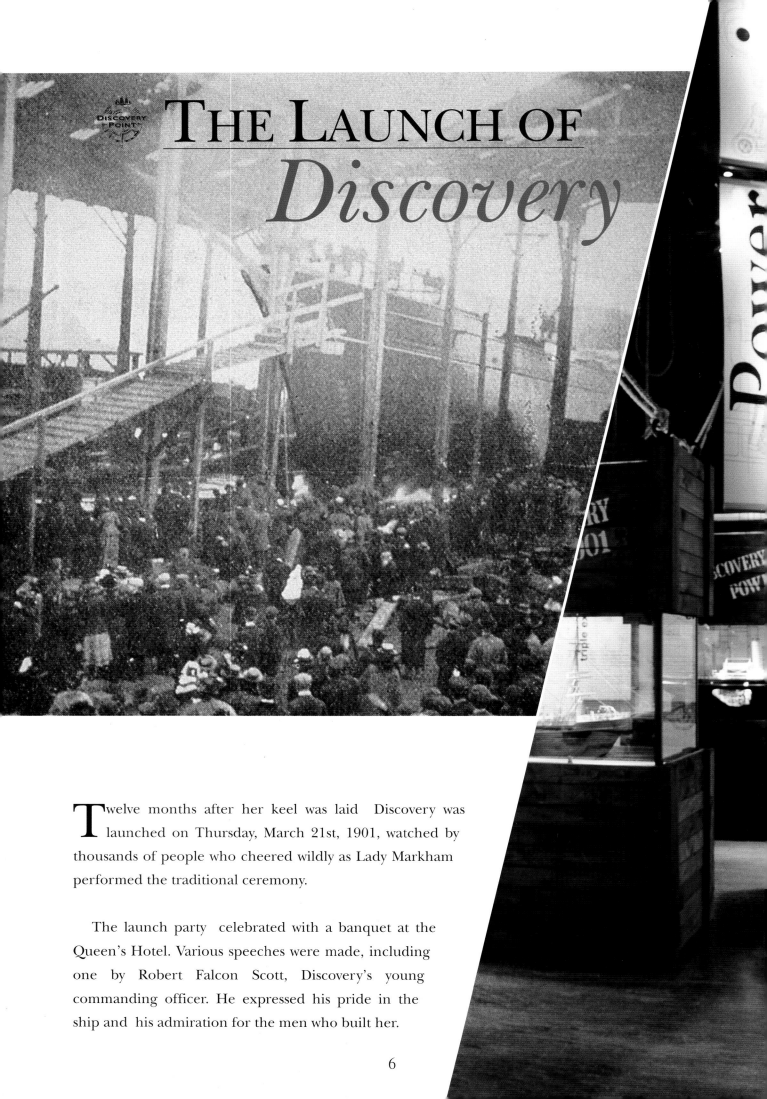

Twelve months after her keel was laid Discovery was launched on Thursday, March 21st, 1901, watched by thousands of people who cheered wildly as Lady Markham performed the traditional ceremony.

The launch party celebrated with a banquet at the Queen's Hotel. Various speeches were made, including one by Robert Falcon Scott, Discovery's young commanding officer. He expressed his pride in the ship and his admiration for the men who built her.

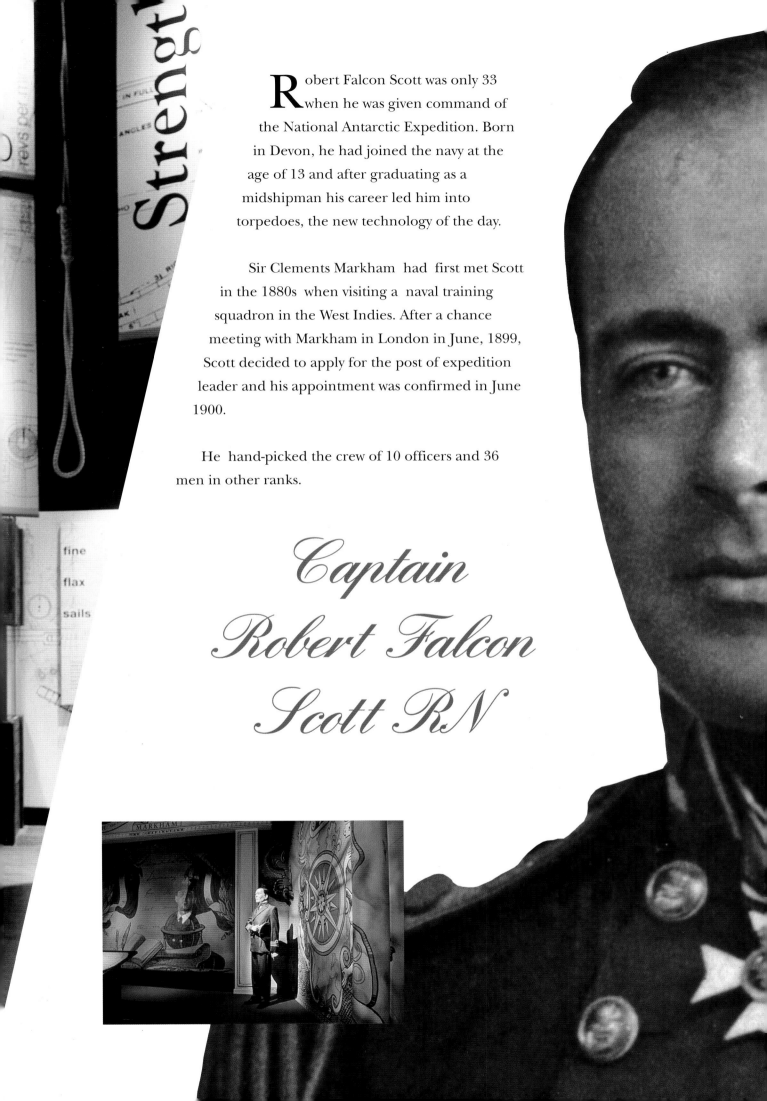

Robert Falcon Scott was only 33 when he was given command of the National Antarctic Expedition. Born in Devon, he had joined the navy at the age of 13 and after graduating as a midshipman his career led him into torpedoes, the new technology of the day.

Sir Clements Markham had first met Scott in the 1880s when visiting a naval training squadron in the West Indies. After a chance meeting with Markham in London in June, 1899, Scott decided to apply for the post of expedition leader and his appointment was confirmed in June 1900.

He hand-picked the crew of 10 officers and 36 men in other ranks.

Captain Robert Falcon Scott RN

PLANS AND PREPARATIONS

Scott supervised the overall planning of the expedition. As well as food, there was the question of clothing, both tropical and polar, sledges, skis, boots, ice equipment, explosives for breaking up ice, personal possessions such as soap, medicines, scientific instruments, a photographic laboratory, furniture, heating oil, a library, balloon equipment, dogs, huts for the expedition, stores for the carpenter, stores for the engineer – the lists seemed endless.

Many firms, with an eye on publicity, supplied goods free. Cadburys sent two tons of cocoa powder, while Colmans supplied barrels of flour and cases of mustard. Bird & Sons contributed huge quantities of their famous custard powder and gallons of lime juice were offered by Evans, Lesher & Webb.

Tobacco was high on the list, almost every man smoked, (Scott himself was never without a pipe or cigar) so 1,800lbs of tobacco were dutifully ordered. In June 1901 Discovery left Dundee for the East India Docks on the Thames where loading of stores began.

On July 31st Discovery sailed from London. The vessel was swung for the

adjustments of her compasses at Spithead and moored off the Isle of Wight during the celebrated Royal Regatta week at Cowes. King Edward V11 and Queen Alexandra came on board on August 5th and inspected the ship. Queen Alexandra even tested the bunks for softness. Next morning the ship sailed.

FOOD · CLOTHING · SKIS · EXPLOSIVES

The Great Adventure was about to begin

The Journey to New Zealand

Discovery's voyage to Antarctica took her down the Atlantic Ocean where the rolling waters were a good test for her new engine. "The ship proves in all respects a wonderfully good sea boat," wrote Scott. A short stop was made at Macquarie Island, about 600 miles south west of New Zealand where the crew collected samples of flora and penguin eggs. Penguin was served for dinner and penguin eggs for breakfast.

Tragedy

The ship was given a great send off in New Zealand by crowds lining the quays and wharves. As the bands played and steamers tooted, a high-spirited young seaman called Charles Bonner climbed above the crow's nest to the top of the mainmast to wave to the cheering crowds. Suddenly he fell, hurtling down head first onto the iron deckhouse. Death was instantaneous.

The loss of the likable young man saddened the crew but Scott was realistic enough to know the gloom would be dispelled by the high level of activity on the ship.

Stopover in New Zealand

Discovery berthed in Lyttelton Harbour, New Zealand on November 29th, 1901. She was restocked and some stores had to be replaced due to being damaged by a leak. This leak became known as the "Dundee leak" and the ship's cook later complained that the labels on some of his tinned food became spoiled by water and he never knew what he was opening. By December 21st Discovery was ready to sail. She was crammed with stores – packing cases even had to be stacked on the deck along with 45 terrified sheep, a present from the farmers of New Zealand, and 23 excited, howling dogs.

ALLOON · DOGS · MUSTARD · TOBACCO

NEW ZEALAND TO ANTARCTICA

On Christmas Eve, 1901, Discovery set sail south towards Antarctica. Fine weather allowed the ship to make good progress and the first iceberg was sighted on January 2nd. On January 3rd, the Antarctic Circle was crossed and for the next five days Discovery pushed her way through 270 miles of pack ice. On January 8th she reached open sea and the first sight of Antarctica's gleaming ice cliffs.

During the next few weeks she sailed eastward along the coastline of the Ross Ice Shelf, taking surveys of the ice cliffs and soundings.

The First Flight over Antarctica

Scott decided it was time to return westwards and look for winter quarters. On the way a bay in the ice shelf was discovered and the ship was able to lie alongside.

The army had supplied the expedition with a balloon known as "Eva", with the request that aerial photographs of the new continent be taken. As "Eva" rose unsteadily to a height of 700 feet, Scott swayed in the shaky basket privately regretting his decision "somewhat selfishly", he admitted later, to be the first man to go up in a balloon over Antarctica.

Once his feet were back on the ground he gladly allowed Shackleton to go up and take photographs.

Winter Quarters

On February 8th, 1902 Discovery anchored in an ice-filled inlet known as McMurdo Sound on the north east side of Ross Island. This sheltered, natural harbour offered protection from icebergs and seemed the ideal base to begin exploring the mainland.

Living Quarters

The first task was to erect the huts. A prefabricated hut intended as living quarters was erected, but in the event the men continued to live on board Discovery and the hut was used as a store, recreation room and workroom.

Two observation huts were also erected. These had to be placed some distance from the ship to avoid any influence from the ship's magnetic metals on the observations. Kennels were provided for the huskies but these hardy dogs preferred to curl up in the snow.

The ship itself was partly covered with an awning of canvas which had been cut, sewn and grommeted in Dundee. This was rigged and lashed overhead to cover the forward part of the deck.

L·O·C·K·E·D

The area surrounding the winter quarters was explored and names such as Castle Point and Crater Rock were given to various landmarks. The crew learned to ski and even played football on the flat ice.

Thomas Hodgson, the Marine Biologist of the Ship's Company, collected fish and other marine life both on the voyage and in Antarctica. When the Discovery reports were written, 5 volumes and 23 expert authors were required to describe the specimens which he found.

He was a world-renowned authority on the sea-spiders collected by the early Antarctic expeditions and returned to work at Plymouth Museum after the expedition.

in T·H·E I·C·E

Sledging parties went out to give the men experience of using the sledges. By the end of March the sea ice began to close in around Discovery and soon she was frozen in from astern.

She was to remain in this position, locked in ice, for two years........

Ferrar plotted the distribution of the different types of rock found in the mountains, recording his observations in detailed scale drawings. The samples he collected contain fossil plants of great scientific value.

THE DARK WINTER

During the Antarctic winter, the sun disappears below the horizon from April to August. A curtain of darkness descends, heightening the feeling of desolation. Scott knew the importance of keeping his men occupied and a busy daily routine was organised. Ice had to be collected on a daily basis for the ship's water supply. Repairs were attended to – sledges, tents, clothing, awnings, ice axes – everything had to be in good order. Clearing the snow from the ship was another priority. Tons of weight on the deck could not be allowed, although drifting snow round the sides of the vessel was left as insulation.

Hunting parties were sent to kill seals and penguins for fresh meat; fish holes were made; the dogs had to be looked after. Some of the men were instructed to help the scientists collect specimens of marine life. Dr Wilson was continually dissecting penguins and seals. He used one of the Wardroom's overhead beams close to the stove as a defrosting shelf for penguins he wished to dissect.

Pastimes

The officers' Wardroom was a crowded place. Looking at it today it's hard to imagine 10 men living there, working, dining, hanging up laundry and smoking. In the evenings the men amused themselves with woodcarving, (one of the carvings can be seen in the Wardroom on board Discovery) reading, writing up diaries, writing letters, debates, concert parties, chess and card games. On the messdeck the rich, heavy aroma of Navy shag permeated the atmosphere as the crew played shove ha'penny, read, repaired clothes, carved or constructed wooden models. Ernest Shackleton produced a ship's magazine once a month called The South Polar Times and invited contributions from the crew and officers. He set up an office in one of the coal bunkers. Contributions included drawings from Dr Wilson, daily experiences, scientific news, information about clothing and theatre news. From time to time plays were performed in one of the huts.

14

Christmas in June

To keep morale up, it was decided to celebrate Christmas on Midwinter's Day, the 21st June. The ship was decorated and some crew members delved into the hold to find the Christmas puddings and cakes that had not been served due to Bonner's death.

Fresh mutton was served along with kidney beans and potatoes and a tot of rum was issued. Presents which Mrs Royds and Mrs Wilson had sent were given out to the men. The day was considered a great success.

cakes each day and fruit tarts. Breakfast was usually porridge with bread, butter, marmalade or jam with seal's liver replacing porridge twice a week. Signs of scurvy meant that seal meat had to be served often, at one point every day. Lunch for the men was their main meal of the day and consisted of soup, meat and a fruit tart. They would have a lighter meal at 5.00pm while the officers ate their main meal at 6.00pm .

A special treat on Sundays was roast mutton. Scott conducted a Sunday service for all on the mess deck. There was even music to accompany the singing, thanks to the American reed harmonium gifted to the ship by the people of New Zealand.

The Question of Food

Feeding 47 men meant that Discovery had left New Zealand laden with ample stores. The problem lay in varying the menus. One cook had already been sacked in New Zealand but his replacement, Brett, proved to be worse and had to be clapped in irons for a while.

The new cook, Charles Clarke, took his job seriously. He tried to bake fresh bread and

ATTEMPT ON THE POLE

A s the sun began to return and the days lengthened, thoughts turned to sledging expeditions and a possible assault on the Pole.

At the beginning of November, the Southern Party, consisting of Scott, Wilson and Shackleton, was ready to explore further south than any man had been before. They estimated they would be away for two to three months and set off in high spirits with nineteen dogs and five sledges of supplies.

The trip turned out to be a gruelling test of the powers of endurance. Progress was painfully slow and only two weeks after leaving the ship, some of the dogs began to die. In some places the terrain changed from smooth, flat ice into frozen furrows and ridges which meant the dogs were unable to pull the sledges, forcing the party to put on harnesses and man-haul the sledges.

It was exhausting, grinding work, but they pushed ahead and on November 25th, in great elation, they passed latitude 80°. Their charts showed only plain white space beyond this point....now they were discovering and recording new land with each day.

WEDDELL SEA

ANTARCTIC PENINSULA

COATES LAND

PALMER LAND

ELLSWORTH LAND

MARIE BYRD LAND

Ice Shel

The Southern Party, left to right: Shackleton, Scott and Wilson
Their route on the map is marked in black

The Turning Point

But physically and psychologically all three men were suffering. The dogs were unable to pull all the sledges, so stores were jettisoned and rations cut. They were hallucinating about food. Frostbite, the dreaded scurvy and snowblindness were in evidence. Wilson, in particular, suffered severe and painful snowblindness, caused by shedding his goggles when sketching the dazzling, white landscapes. Tensions between Scott and Shackleton surfaced. Shackleton did not agree with some of Scott's decisions and could not hide his feelings. Scott resented his authority being questioned. As more dogs were reduced to a pitiable state, they had to be killed and the meat fed to the surviving dogs to keep them going. At a latitude of 82°17', some 530 miles from the Pole, they turned for home.

Shackleton was now in the advanced stages of scurvy, coughing up blood and no longer capable of carrying anything. The last two dogs were killed and the final, dreary trudge began. Finally on February 3rd, after 93 days and over 950 miles, they were within 6 miles of the ship when they were met by Skelton and Bernacchi who brought the joyful news that the relief ship Morning had arrived.

KING HAAKON VII
SEA

DRONNG
MAUD
LAND

ENDERBY
LAND

KEMP LAND

MAC-
ROBERTSON
LAND

PRINCESS
ELIZABETH
LAND

South Pole

Last Depot
1½ Degree Depot
Evans retd.
3 Degree Depot
Atkinson retd.

WILHELM II
LAND

QUEEN MARY
LAND

Southern Party's
furthest point
30-12-02

WILKES
LAND

Meares retd.
Evans died
Blizzard

Day retd.

Oates
Tent
Bluff Depot

VICTORIA
LAND

Safety Camp

ROSS
SEA

TERRE
ADELIE

GEORGE V
LAND

OATES LAND

DUMONT d'URVILLE SEA

Scott described the joy of seeing "our beloved ship". In his absence Discovery had been prepared for the open sea and freshly painted. In the event the ship was to remain locked in ice for another winter. Efforts to free her using dynamite failed, and eventually the relief ship Morning sailed, unwilling to end up locked in ice herself.

Shackleton's Departure

Ernest Shackleton and several other men were invalided home with the Morning on Scott's insistence. This was a bitter blow to Shackleton's pride. He felt Scott was looking for an excuse to get rid of him and he vowed he would be back. He became obsessed with the idea of being the first man to reach the Pole.

The Second Winter

As the expedition settled down to a second winter in the Antarctic, Scott began to plan a trip to the polar plateau. In October 1903 a six-man team set off onto Ferrar Glacier. There were no dogs, so each man had to haul his own sledge and it was soul destroying. The party split on November 22, with Scott, Lashly and Evans continuing on up the glacier to 9000 feet. They emerged onto the polar plateau...and could only gaze in awe at the vast dome of ice, stretching from sea to sea and covering the bottom of the world. Weather conditions deteriorated into a nightmare..... blizzards, biting wind and sub-zero temperatures made progress painfully slow as they retraced their steps. They trudged on in grim determination and reached Discovery on December 3rd.

ESCAPE FROM *THE* ICE

The crew of the Terra Nova

There was depressing news as far as the release of Discovery was concerned. There were now 20 miles of ice, 8 feet thick in places, between the ship and the open sea. Scott began to contemplate the possibility that he might have to spend a third winter in Antarctica.

In January 5th, 1904, he received a welcome surprise with the arrival of the relief ship Morning and also the Terra Nova, a Scottish steam whaler. The relief was to be bitter sweet, however, when Captain William Colbeck of the Morning and Captain Harry MacKay of Terra Nova told him that if Discovery could not be freed by the end of February, she would have to be abandoned. The expedition had run out of funds and the Admiralty was not prepared to finance any more relief or rescue operations.

It was decided that controlled explosions around the ship were the best option to free her. These continued until February when the ice began to break up naturally. Finally, on February 16th, the ship was free.

Captain Harry MacKay and Terra Nova

The Terra Nova was the last whaler to be built in Dundee. Launched in 1884, she spent many years operating around Newfoundland and the Davis Straits. In 1903 she was bought by the Government to assist in the rescue of Discovery from the Antarctic ice and was sent for an urgent refit to Dundee. The Dundee Shipbuilding Company put 300 men to work and the repairs, re-fit and re-rigging were completed in 14 days. She was placed under the command of Dundee-born Captain Harry MacKay, a veteran of the whaling fleet, and a man who knew the dangers of navigating in polar waters. After his part in rescuing Discovery, he returned to whaling and sealing until retiring in 1909.

The Terra Nova was to achieve lasting fame as the ship which carried Scott on his last, ill-fated polar expedition of 1910-13. Afterwards, she resumed her sealing career in Newfoundland but was lost in Canadian waters in 1943.

*OFFICERS AND MEMBERS OF THE SCIENTIFIC STAFF ON BOARD
DISCOVERY, 1901
Left to Right: Wilson, Shackleton, Armitage, Barne, Koettlitz, Skelton, Scott,
Royds, Bernacchi, Ferrar, Hodgson*

Discovery arrived back at Spithead on September 10th, 1904. She carried men who had lived for 26 months at the edge of the world's most inhospitable continent ...men who had penetrated further into the unknown white wilderness than anyone before them. They were heroes.

Scott was given a rapturous reception and told his story to a packed crowd from the stage of the Albert Hall, flanked by the flags his sledges had carried.

The second attempt on the Pole

Robert Falcon Scott remained fascinated by Antarctica. He desperately wanted to be the first man to explore its heart, the South Pole, and in 1910 he announced he would lead a second expedition. 8,000 men volunteered to join him. Discovery was not available to him so he used the Terra Nova. The expedition was to become a human tragedy of classical proportions – Scott and four companions reached the Pole only to discover that the Norwegian Amundsen had beaten them by just over a month.

Scott and his team now faced a gruelling 800-mile trek back to the Terra Nova. Frustrated and sick at heart, they were hit by ferocious blizzards and progress was slow. Food ran perilously low. Petty Officer Evans died after a bad fall and Lieutenant Oates, realising he was holding back his companions because of his badly frostbitten feet, opened the tent flap one morning and walked out, saying "I'm just going outside...and I may be some time".

His sacrifice was in vain. Scott, Dr Wilson and Lieutenant Bowers died in their tent, just 11 miles from the next food depot. Their bodies were found 8 months later and left undisturbed. There they lie today, entombed 50 feet or more beneath the mantle of snow accumulating on the Ross Ice Shelf.

"I'm just going outside ... and I may be some time."

Lieutenant Oates

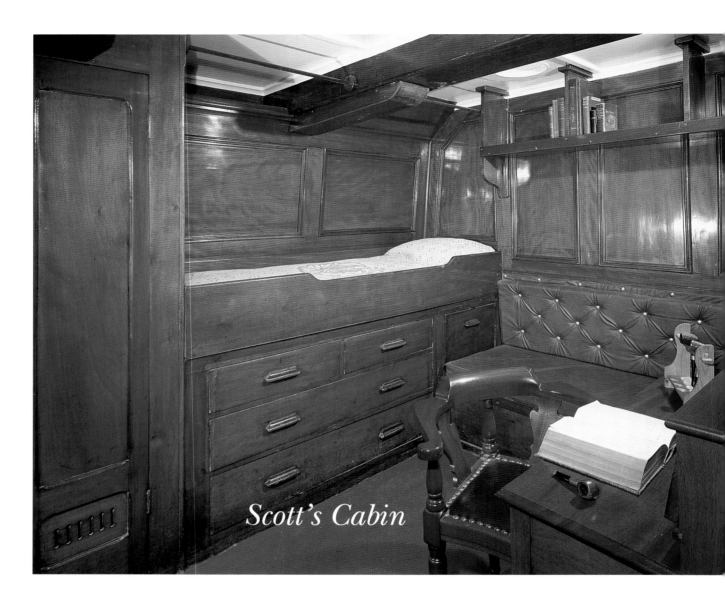

Scott's Cabin

'Frozen in time'

Left:
The harmonium given to the crew in 1901 by the
people of Christchurch in New Zealand

Below:
A woodcarving done by a crew member
during the 1901–1904 expedition, now on
display in the Wardroom

What now for Discovery?

It was hoped she could continue as a scientific research vessel but the National Antarctic Expedition was in dire financial straits and the ship was sold to the Hudson's Bay Company in January, 1905, for a fifth of her builder's price.

The company wanted the ship because of her ability to break through ice. She was converted into a cargo vessel and spent the years between 1905 and 1911 carrying supplies to Hudson's Bay in Northern Canada and returning mostly with furs.

During World War 1 she ran munitions to Russia under charter to the French government and in 1917 she carried supplies to the White Russians via the Black Sea during the Russian Revolution. At the end of the war she was chartered by a number of companies for merchant work in the North Atlantic.

Between 1920 and 1922, Discovery lay idle in the South West India Docks in London. Her limited cargo capacity and speed meant she could not compete with modern merchant ships. She was laid up and became temporary headquarters of the 16th Stepney Sea Scout Troop.

Back to Antarctica

But Discovery's days of exploration were not yet over. In 1923 she was bought by the Crown Agents for the Colonies for the purpose of scientific research in the South Seas and given a major refit at the Vospers ship repair yard in Gosport, Hants.

Refit 1923-24

The cost of the purchase and reconstruction of Discovery, excluding scientific equipment, was almost £114,000. The refit included:-

Changes to the sails and rigging
New masts of Oregon pine
Hull re-planked, inside and out
New decks
New deckhouses
Chemical & biological laboratories
Winches, powered reels,
Sounding machines,
Outboard platforms

Her place of registration was changed from London to Port Stanley, Falklands and she was designated a Royal Research Ship.

In October 1925 she sailed for the South Seas on an expedition to research the migration pattern of whales and whale stocks.

The B.A.N.Z.A.R. Expeditions

The British, Australian and New Zealand Antarctic Expedition (known as B.A.N.Z.A.R.E.) began in 1929 under the leadership of Sir Douglas Mawson. The British Government agreed to lend Discovery free of charge to the expedition.

The expedition's brief was to chart coasts, islands, rocks and shoals between Queen Mary Land and Enderby Island and "plant the British flag wherever you find it practicable to do so".

Mawson put together a well-organised scientific team for B.A.N.Z.A.R.E. There was even a Gipsy Moth bi-plane to do aerial survey work. Landing parties were made and several chunks of land were claimed on behalf of the British Government. Discovery returned to Australia in April, 1930 where she was overhauled. She then set sail for a second B.A.N.Z.A.R. expedition. Again much valuable scientific work was done. New areas were discovered and charted and she brought back masses of geological and zoological samples.

1931 – 1986

Discovery's days as a research ship were now over. She was laid up in the London docks and in 1936 she was given to the Boy Scouts Association as a training ship for Sea Scouts and as a memorial to Captain Scott. During World War 2 the Royal Navy used her for training purposes. In the later years of the war her engine and boilers were removed and sent for scrap

With the passing years the Scouts found the upkeep of Discovery too costly and in 1955 she was transferred to the Admiralty for use by the Royal Naval Auxiliary Reserve as a drill ship. She was open to the public at the weekends.

Her condition was steadily deteriorating, however, and in the late 1970s a question mark hung over her future. The Ministry of Defence felt the huge cost of essential repairs could not be justified. The Maritime Trust stepped in and in April, 1979 the ship was formerly taken into its care. Vital restoration work began and she became a national museum and tourist attraction on the River Thames.

The Maritime Trust

The Maritime Trust was established in 1969. The aim of the Trust is to preserve and restore Britain's historic ships and put them on show to the public. The Trust is an independent charity and receives no government subsidy.

Between 1979 and 1985 half a million pounds was spent by the Maritime Trust on the first stage of Discovery's restoration using the Vosper re-fit plans.

Home to Dundee!

In 1985 a new home was offered to Discovery by Dundee Heritage Trust in partnership with the Scottish Development Agency. The ship could return to the city where she had been built and eventually be the centre-piece of a new heritage centre. The ship left London on March 28th, 1986 as dry cargo in the Happy Mariner. She was too precious to risk being towed in the choppy waters

of the North Sea. Reaching the estuary of the River Tay she was greeted by thousands of Dundonians who cheered as she made her way up the river. At midnight on April 3rd Discovery finally berthed in Victoria Dock. A piper appeared on her deck and a pipe band on the quayside played songs of welcome.

H·O·M·E A·T L·A·S·T

*I*n 1992 Discovery was moved a short distance upriver to her own custom-built dock, to become an integral part of Discovery Point, Dundee's flagship tourist attraction. HRH Prince Philip opened the new award-winning centre on July 1, 1993.

RESTORATION

Since Discovery returned to Dundee a major programme of restoration has been undertaken by Dundee Heritage Trust.

This has included replacement of some of the ship's outer and inner planking, replacement of the lower masts and the replacement of the stem and stern posts. She has been re-wired for lighting and power. A ventilation system and electrically-operated bilge pumps have been installed.

Discovery has been dry-docked twice and new technologies in ship restoration, such as the steam sterilisation of infected timbers,

Below: Work on the restoration of Discovery's timbers nears completion. Due to conservation measures new woods such as Opepe are sometimes used in place of Elm, Pitch Pine and Greenheart. The Maritime Trust supervised all the restoration work.

have been carried out by the Imperial College of Science, Technology and Medicine in London. Some of these treatments are firsts in ship restoration and have attracted international interest.

Aboard, the officers' cabins and the Chart Room have been restored. Plans are in hand to restore the Wireless Room, Captain's Day Cabin and the Sick Bay.

The Maritime Trust continued to own Discovery until 1995 when it was agreed to transfer ownership to Dundee Heritage Trust for the princely sum of £1. A one pound note dating from 1901, the year of Discovery's launch, was handed over to conclude the bargain!

The Chartroom

DISCOVERY POINT

Souvenir Shop

The shop on the Point carries a wide range of quality gifts in all price ranges. Many items are exclusive to Discovery Point.

Cafe on the Point

The Cafe and Gallery on the Point serves morning coffees, snacks, light lunches and afternoon teas. A changing programme of exhibitions allows visitors to buy original artwork by talented local artists.

Education Services

School parties of all ages are welcome at Discovery Point. There are two fully-equipped Education Suites (one a converted coal bunker on board RRS Discovery!) where children can participate in pre-arranged activities, project work and eat their packed lunches. A comprehensive education pack is available and teachers are invited to book a complimentary reconnaissance visit prior to their school trip.

Conference Facilities

Discovery Point is the city centre venue with a difference. Comfortable facilities, a warm welcome and stunning views of Discovery and the River Tay make Discovery Point ideal for functions and conferences for up to 200 people. On board ship the lavish mahogany and brass of the Wardroom create a wonderful atmosphere for an intimate dinner party (maximum 14) for very special guests.

BLUE-EYED SHAGS are a relative of our European cormorants and shags. They are to be found on the Antarctic peninsular

In spite of its inhospitable climate, the Antarctic continent sustains a variety of unique wildlife. Millions of penguins on its icy verges, albatross, petrel and skua gulls glide overhead while the icy seas offer home to many species of seals, the savage sea leopard, killer whales and the magnificent blue whale.

One man keenly interested in the preservation of Antarctica's unique environment was Sir Peter Scott, son of Captain Scott. "Make the boy interested in nature. It's better than games . . ." wrote Scott before setting off on his last Antarctic expedition in 1910. Peter Scott went on to change the world's attitude to nature and ecology. He played a vital part in establishing the World Wildlife Fund and strove to ensure that the riches of Antarctica, particularly its wildlife, should be regarded as common heritage, to be enjoyed by all mankind and preserved for future generations.

The LEOPARD SEAL'S main source of food is the penguin. The female seal can grow up to 10ft in length

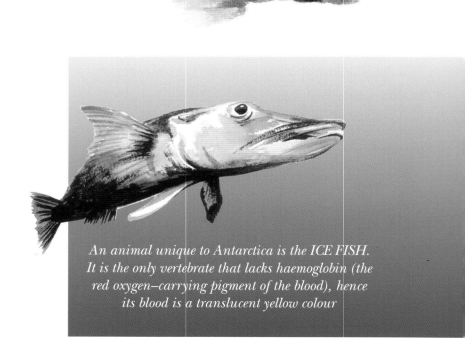

An animal unique to Antarctica is the ICE FISH. It is the only vertebrate that lacks haemoglobin (the red oxygen–carrying pigment of the blood), hence its blood is a translucent yellow colour

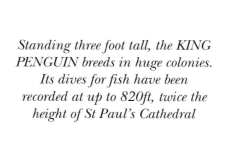

Standing three foot tall, the KING PENGUIN breeds in huge colonies. Its dives for fish have been recorded at up to 820ft, twice the height of St Paul's Cathedral

The ELEPHANT SEAL is the largest of all seals in the southern hemisphere. The male has an inflatable 'trunk' which it uses to scare away potential rivals. Battles between males can be awesome spectacles

There are 7 species of penguin in the Antarctic. This CHINSTRAP PENGUIN is the smallest of the 'brush-tailed' species. Its population is estimated at 10 million and increasing

The ORCA, aptly named the KILLER WHALE, is the largest of all carnivores. It feeds on seals and penguins, sometimes ramming icebergs to knock its prey into the water.

The FIN WHALE is the second largest animal on earth next to the Blue Whale. It remains north of the ice-edge and feeds on krill and plankton

DUNDEE HERITAGE TRUST

Dundee Heritage Trust was formed in January 1985 to preserve and present Dundee's industrial past. Trustees are drawn from a diverse range of community and business interests in Dundee and Tayside and the Trust has been generously supported by public bodies, local industry and individual benefactors.

The restoration of RRS Discovery and the opening of Discovery Point in 1993 were the culmination of many years effort by Dundee Heritage Trust. The Trust is currently establishing a living museum of textiles at Verdant Works, a 19th century linen and jute mill in the heart of what was the city's main textile area. This exciting visitor centre brings back memories of Dundee's long connections with the spinning of flax and jute with working machinery, state of the art exhibitions and children's interactive displays. The Trust has an active membership of volunteer Friends who provide invaluable help both aboard Discovery and at Verdant Works.

For all enquiries contact
Dundee Heritage Trust
Verdant Works
West Hendersons Wynd
Dundee DD2 5BT

Telephone: (01382) 225282
Fax: (01382) 221612

Acknowledgments

Text by Margaret Hunter

Photographs by Alex Coupar, Hugh Scott, Peter Kinnear, Nina Finnigan, The Valentine Collection, University of St. Andrews, Dundee City Council and Royal Geographical Society

Antarctic map, Union ensign and wildlife paintings by Nick McCann

Dundee Industrial Heritage Ltd
Registered in Scotland 93109
Registered Charity Number: ED/343/85 PLB

ISBN   1 874670 28 5

Designed and published by Pilgrim Press Ltd.,
Heritage House, Lodge Lane, Derby DE1 3HE and printed in Great Britain.
Telephone: (01332) 347087. Fax: (01332) 290688